NASCAR Champions

KYLE BUSCH

Connor Dayton

PowerKiDS press.

New York

Published in 2008 by The Rosen Publishing Group, Inc.
29 East 21st Street, New York, NY 10010

First Edition

Editor: Jennifer Way
Book Design: Michael J. Flynn
Layout Design: Kate Laczynski
Photo Researcher: Nicole Pristash

Photo Credits: All images © Getty Images.

Library of Congress Cataloging-in-Publication Data

Dayton, Connor.
  Kyle Busch / Connor Dayton. — 1st ed.
      p. cm. — (Nascar champions)
  Includes index.
  ISBN-13: 978-1-4042-3817-6 (library binding)
  ISBN-10: 1-4042-3817-4 (library binding)
  1. Busch, Kyle—Juvenile literature. 2. Stock car drivers—United States—Biography—Juvenile literature. I. Title.
  GV1032.B87D39b 2008
  796.72092—dc22
  [B]
                                        2007005431

Manufactured in the United States of America

Contents

Kyle Busch was born May 2, 1985, in Las Vegas, Nevada. He has been racing since he was very young.

Some people call Kyle Busch Kyle Shrub. A shrub is a little bush. This is a play on his name and the fact that he is a younger brother of fellow racer Kurt Busch.

Kyle Busch began racing in the Craftsman Truck **Series** in 2001, when he was 16 years old. This is a young age to start racing.

When Kyle Busch was 18, he began racing in NASCAR's Busch Series. He did so well that he was named that series' 2003 **Rookie** of the Year.

10

11

In 2005, Busch became part of the Hendrick Motorsports team. He also moved up to the Nextel Cup Series that year.

12

Busch's first **season** in the Nextel Cup Series went very well. He was even named Rookie of the Year for the second time in his racing **career**!

14

Kyle Busch drives a Chevrolet Monte Carlo on the Hendrick team. Two of the team's biggest **sponsors** are Pepsi and Lowe's.

16

Kyle Busch likes to spend time with his family when he is not racing. He looks up to Kurt, who Kyle says has taught him a lot about being a great driver.

18

19

Kyle Busch finished in tenth place in his second season in the Nextel Cup. This is a good **ranking**. Busch hopes to have a long career in NASCAR.

Glossary

career (KUH-reer) A job.

ranking (RAN-king) A measure of how well a player is doing in a sport.

rookie (RU-kee) A new player or driver.

season (SEE-zun) The group of games or races for a year.

series (SIR-eez) A group of races.

sponsors (SPON-serz) People or groups that pay for someone else, such as a racer.

Books and Web Sites

Books

Kelley, K.C. *NASCAR Daring Drivers*. Pleasantville, NY: Reader's Digest, 2005.

Schaefer, Adam R. *Racing with the Pit Crew*. Mankato, MN: Capstone Press, 2006.

Web Sites

Due to the changing nature of Internet links, the Rosen Publishing Group, Inc., has developed an online list of Web sites related to the subject of this book. This site is updated regularly. Please use this link to access the list: www.powerkidslinks.com/nas/kbus/

23

Index